# Because of You

*Palewell Press*

# Because of You

*Selected Poems – Bilal Al Masri translated from Arabic by Dr Anba Jawi MBE and Dr Mohamad Haj Mohamad*

Because of You

First edition 2024 from Palewell Press, www.palewellpress.co.uk

Printed and bound in the UK

ISBN 978-1-911587-74-3

All Rights Reserved. Copyright © 2024 Bilal Al Masri. No part of this publication may be reproduced or transmitted in any form or by any means, without permission in writing from the author. The right of Bilal Al Masri to be identified as the author of this work and of Dr Anba Jawi MBE and Dr Mohamad Haj Mohamad to be identified as its translators has been asserted by them in accordance with the Copyright, Designs and Patents Act 1988

The cover design is Copyright © 2024 Camilla Reeve

The front cover image is Copyright © 2024 Safa'a S. Iskandar  safaaiskandar23@gmail.com

The back cover photo of Bilal Al Masri is Copyright © 2024 Bilal Al Masri

A CIP catalogue record for this title is available from the British Library.

# Acknowledgements

All of the translated poems in this collection were originally published in Arabic.

# Contents

Introduction ..................................................... 2
Editor's Note about the Translation ................ 5
A Story ............................................................ 6
Please Be Cherishing ..................................... 8
Be Sympathetic .............................................. 9
I love you ...................................................... 10
Follow Me ..................................................... 12
Without Me ................................................... 13
Darkness ...................................................... 14
The Path ....................................................... 15
Squabbles .................................................... 16
Whiteness .................................................... 17
Music Track .................................................. 18
Absence ....................................................... 19
My Mother .................................................... 20
The Ring ...................................................... 21
The Witch ..................................................... 22
Maturity ........................................................ 23
Tears ............................................................ 24
Jasmine rises like bullets ............................. 25
And because of you… .................................. 30

What has the violin done to you? ...... 33
The Treasure ...... 35
Until you have become a garden ...... 36
Exercise ...... 42
Sparrow ...... 43
Words ...... 44
With Me ...... 45
BILAL AL MASRI – POET ...... 47
DR ANBA JAWI, MBE – TRANSLATOR & EDITOR ...... 48
DR MOHAMAD HAJ MOHAMAD – TRANSLATOR ...... 49

-

# SELECTED POEMS
# BY BILAL AL MASRI
# TRANSLATED FROM ARABIC

# Introduction

I was in the middle of working on another translation project when Camilla asked me to have a look at Bilal's poems. She sent me an initial translation by Dr M H Mohamad and the original copy in Arabic.

There is always a choice in making a new poem in another language from the original version. It is a new poem, because it is impossible, in poetry, to be exact. Translators can stay close to the original, or they can wander, sometimes quite far.

Working with both versions, my job as an editor was to pull the poems closer to what felt like an accurate representation of the work. It was a triangulation of meanings that took months to complete. I'd like to thank Dr M H Mohamad for his first version.

Bilal's poems consist of many layers and translating them into English was, at times, tricky. I would talk to Bilal on many occasions asking him, "what do you mean by this line, because this word means this and this and the following word's meaning is the opposite."

Then I understood his observations of his surroundings, which sound simple and yet are very complex. He touches the edge of Sufism yet you think he is writing about Nihilism. Sometimes, he leaves you on a cliff-hanger.

Through this he picks up all the contradictions of life, humanity, his city and his country. He digs deep into a beautiful yet harsh reality, possibly because he is living in a country torn by wars, where human life has no value, and killing is ordinary.

"Dead or killed it makes no difference, but I killed you."

It is this harsh reality that made Bilal use his language and words to create a surge in feeling, showing contradictions and clashes to an astonishing level.

Bilal is an ace at using the literary device of oxymoron and paradox. He simply uses them brilliantly.

"I carry my head with cut off hands."

The reader will find that Bilal writes about presence and absence, life and death, existence and nothingness, blackness and whiteness. These dualities are expressed in amazing antonyms.

Working with Camilla was a stimulating and rewarding experience and I thank her for introducing such a unique voice to the English reader.

**Dr. Anba Jawi, MBE**
**January 2024**

# Editor's Note about the Translation

Translating poetry is said to be one of the most challenging of literary tasks. Typically, it requires several stages with different language and literary specialists involved at each stage.

Palewell Press would like to acknowledge the team involved in rendering Bilal Al-Masri's selected poems from the original Arabic text into English poetry for their first UK publication – Dr. Anba Jawi MBE, Dr M H Mohamad, Camilla Reeve at Palewell Press, and Bilal Al-Masri himself for answering their many questions about the text.

**Camilla Reeve**

# A Story

1.
Like smoke dispersing,
words distance themselves
as you and I return to being strangers

just two characters lost in a long story,
an endless one, whose sad author
is uncertain which way to turn

2.
When you are writing, remember to be gentle
to passers-by within the story. They pass, by chance,
like a woman throws herself beneath a train
or a flower withers in a book

All of them have souls
which they would gladly sacrifice
to help the story's heroes to survive
and climb the words up to the very end

3.
At story's end, the lovers will find their way
and comprehend their unique story

Let their hearts sing a song of eagerness,
let them touch each other
as a plant reaches for the sun

It is alright to wither flowers in a book
or for a woman to throw herself beneath a train –
tortured souls seeking liberation from their bodies
–
only lovers devour each other's bodies as a sacrament
but do not let them bear children,
this world is not a good one

## Please Be Cherishing

Be warm to all war-orphaned children.
In a war, don't leave them
permanently orphaned.
Fashion pairs of wings
for those who lost their limbs...

Don't ever wave goodbye to them
but smile and let your smile follow them
wherever they may go.

## Be Sympathetic

Be sympathetic to the poor,
speak a word to them
which no-one knows but you,
build houses for them
in between the lines
to stretch their fragile bodies in,
make your words into their bread
and let them re-inspire you to write stories
with neither thirst nor hunger in them.

## I love you

All your languages, I can understand.
All your complexions resemble mine.
I don't hate you.

Each creature has a beating heart.
We're at the heart of Life
bearing love's pulse within,
both I and you.

Does your advanced science
make you think yourself superior?
If so, you drink of foolishness.

Beware of being certain
you are right. Remember,
if love's light leaves your heart
you will be bound for Hell.

Once there, do something to survive,
become acquainted with terror,
and keep moving forwards
towards peace without barriers.

Call greetings to the wild dogs.
Don't hit them with a stick.
as that is what they want –
to make you be like them,
a merciless monster.

# Follow Me

As waves follow each other
up onto the shore, follow me
Don't trust to sounds.
I am the silence when you're solitary.
Trust in me.

When you are alone
I rise up in your chest and stir you.
Don't ask me who I am.
My purpose is in your heart –
I touch it and leave it
and will not stop until you let me in.

Think about your soul.
Focus on it then let it go.
I will be here until you open up the door.

Emerge from me.
Don't ask me where we're going.
Just follow me.

## Without Me

The sun's chariot moves across the sky
dragging itself along its daily path.
But you are without steps, without a path,
without me, you'll be trappped in darkness.

It is so ironic –
some people think they are just who they are
but they are *what* they are and born of dust.

If you only knew –
this very evening, from dry bread
I made you a full moon.
But even that, without me,
would leave you unsatisfied.

## Darkness

It's hard to totally erase the dark.
Were you to draw a thousand suns
you wouldn't banish darkness.
Truly it's a melancholy song.

So set aside your ego,
get over yourself,
don't worry if another defeats you,
give even-handedly to all who hate you
as well as those who love
for Life is nothing but a game.

And everything will disappear.

# The Path

Strangers know
that love can have no home
nor trees to shade it.
For you are walking
through a desert
where one star guides you
and another leads astray
but you are unconcerned –
the route is in your heart.

## Squabbles

The tree's more lovely when it's naked,
seeing through it is more joyful.
Through it, I can watch the sky
wilting on bare boughs.

Like a little child
I can lift the sky up, near or far.

You grown-ups, older people,
you don't know
how we shake each other
like a squabble
between nothingness and being.

## Whiteness

What the snowman wanted to say
before he melted:
Why do one's eyes go white
from sadness,
why does foam vanish irrevocably,
what is this whiteness
that causes blindness?

## Music Track

I'm going to where I can exist
always making sure my feet
stay anchored to the ground,

running my feet along a track,
composing a symphony for life,
for our existence.

But I am sick, so very sick,
as fearful of myself as I fear heights.

# Absence

As meetings with you became rarer
I folded myself between the pages of a book
and went upon my way,

having forgotten I was sick –
your absence pained me –
I could not remember
where I had left the book.

## My Mother

Her silence is a boat,
sea is but a drop upon her palm,
that is how I plan to drown
wrapped in her blue sheets,
swaying, to and fro,
until the universe grows old.

How many waves are you, Mother?
Oh, plenty.
Still I ask, and your silence endures.
That is the answer I love.

In every seashell there's a song –
seagulls are becoming clouds
impossible to separate from sky.
I no longer know what to become
for I have lost my song.

Mother
I dangle from the swing of your silence.
I teach my children
how to handle water
without injuring the waves.

# The Ring

When a ring fell into the water
a Genie of the lake appeared
trapping the poet with her spell.

She had the water make
bracelet-fetters for the poet's hands
so that he grew willing
and happy to surrender.

Seeing swans embrace,
the poet desired their wings.
The Genie fashioned wings for him
but left him crippled.

# The Witch

Her mouth is like a fish
swimming in a bowl of silence.
All I know of her
are images inside my mind,

Bleeding from deep wounds,
I am the only one
whom she did not restore
to how I used to be –

I'm still a tattoo upon her back.
Every time she scratches it
lightning strikes my soul.

# Maturity

Swear words bear fruit
ripening in my head.
My heart rises
as high as yeasty bread
while my limbs dissolve
in an acid-bath of doubt.

Has smoke become my home
or will I choke on it?
Am I swallowing bulldozers
or using them to pave a road?
While this fire gasps,
long-awaited cold awakens
and the peace
for which I waited ages
unravels in my hands.

# Tears

Dogs chase after the Moon.
Spinster cats miaow.
In the dead of night
poor mice hide
in the ear of an old woman,
combing her grey hair,
which falls like snowflakes
and melts like tears.
Meanwhile there are people
wandering along the paths,
crushing each other's hearts.

# Jasmine rises like bullets

The sun rose like a wild-cat,
mewing and coiling round itself.
The sea ran like a child afraid
or someone chasing prey
with its fangs of froth.

I bowed down over darkness
as a shoeshine boy,
holding it in my hands
and sweeping up the stars
instead of garden leaves.

Bread resembles a stab-wound.
A wretched man fled heaven
as Adam, his father,
had left his shoes behind
within the Vale of Earth.

With every step he took
he would shake his stick
to keep from stumbling through waves.
And when wolves bit
into the edge of evening,
night screamed.

The lover jumped
over a garden fence,
fell into a bush of jasmine.
Then jasmine flowers rose up
like a shower of bullets.

Yesterday you were here –
all fire-stippled chestnut,
like the smile of a boy
with wildly curling hair
racing against the wind,
fantasy and hungry shades.
White Buffalo, I was eaten
on the same day as you.
You have so many hands
and I just two.

Now, others hammer
nails into my voice
for I am not a god.
I'm just like you,
seller of luck
at the end of the day,

I lose my dream
at a sharp-edged table
then brag about myelf.

Legs part and sun
beams through the opening
like thousands of creatures
seeking Life's pleasure
and hands arrange the planets:
Saturn, Venus, and Earth.

I say, how great you are, oh Mother.
Her laughter echoes round me
and she answers,
your mother, she is also great.

This rain-storm will not quieten.
It's like a wolf that lost its jaws
in a horrifying accident.
Can you believe it?
This love is not true love –
It merely fills the gap between two faces.
In the photo,
I'm carrying my head in sawn-off hands.

I'm going round in circles,
I'm a random colour
I am the fool, the fool, the fool
to have put you on
and worn you, man.
In the photo.
I'm carrying my head in sawn-off hands
like the end of the road.

Between two strange bodies
I find myself alone
as twelve stray lambs
ask me for the way.

Yes, it is really me.
There is a pleasure in feeling
the nails piercing my hands,
which have forgotten how to signal.

All those I loved are back.
Like a stubborn screech,
one of them cries "I missed you"
and my nailed hands try
to hug one of them. I shiver,
swinging to and fro in my pleasure,

I'm like two lovers, one's in the sky
and the other has not come down.
It's true, this is me.
Him
You
Don't cast stones at my mirrors,
the drowned breathe in his ten commandments.

Yesterday I was there
and the girdle of waters were tolling
Me
He
You
dancing in darkness
that lends our bodies
the longest shadow
in the shortest words.

## And because of you...

Because you are
a vase brimming with perfume
and because you are
a bunch of cherries
ripe as the blood of revolutionaries,
you sway and I fall into yearning.

And because you are
the secret between confidantes,
I nod, you nod.
I'll be the ebb and flow in you
and you will be
the sad heartstrings in me.

And because you are
a gasping in my chest,
wounded by reeds,
I imagine you as if you were
a butterfly embracing flame.

Because you eliminate before and after,
because you're the Garden of Eden in Genesis,
because you wear so many faces,
I think you're both cold and heat,
war and roses, peace and dreaming.

Because you are a flock of doves
soaring in my chest, each time
I try to stop myself exhaling.

Because you are
a violin while it is still hidden
within its mother-tree
I murmur to you.
Because you are
both tender and fresh
yet wilting as a dying rose,
I call on you to pour as rain
brimming in cells and veins.

Because you make
the white things whiter
I rush towards you
like a ringing chord.
Because you are
desirable as falling tears,
pure as lightning
like the rain, I fall on you.

Because
in a desert of nostalgia
you dig for stories,
because you wreck me with desire,
you light fires in my dry grass
and then you leave.

# What has the violin done to you?

I see you
yet I don't see you.
Wherever you are
I am your shadow
and your secret-keeper.

Your hands are the banks
of a river of longing.
What has the violin done to you?
Days enfold each other
like the pages of a book
nibbled by Love's mice.

No time remains for growing older.
Words have already grown old.
Rivulets surface on our faces.
Your hands have started to shake
and you're picking up my heart.

You grew old
without my even noticing,
leaving me still a child
as I was before we met –
chasing after your waves
and drowning in you –

I breathe you.
You are like death.
After you I have no idea
what will happen to me.

# The Treasure

How can I be sure
that language is the treasure
in the hinterland of the soul?

I doubt that balconies –
which dangle from buildings
like the earrings of women –
are the entire city!
Rather the body is the original place
where Time was born.

Sometimes I feel the Earth
is a morsel in the mouth
of the universe –
this predatory being
expanding endlessly,

like paradise is
a search for pure nihilism,
yet that discovery
brings no new knowledge,
just hell growing out of questions.

## Until you have become a garden

I am sitting next to my soul.
I circle around it
like a boy,
a Sufi Sheikh,
a worn-out fan.
But my words lack hands
for holding yours!

Paper boats
loaded with our words
have sunk.
All we ever said
has now become
a stony road.

Stories have gained our wrinkles
because we forgot
that we had written
our names on the trunks of trees.

We have become displaced
like an untended fire
when it dozes
gets smothered by ashes
until our absence
is filling every corner.

Further into our book
a divine rain will fall
and shake the image.

Amazement rides
the horse of silence.

I swing upon your vocal chords,
try to cleanse water
with some of your being.
Let us doze together
in the heart of a fossilised tree,

Like you, I long to die
as a plant would, silently,
let dark drink what is left of us
and my shadow enfold your silhouette
as a silken coat.

I roll the words, I roll them,
backfill their whiteness,
not all the whiteness
just around the eye's small pupil,
and this voice
is fleeing to its broken icon
deep within the mountain.

I gather the directions
and lay them out before you.
I have no beliefs, only you
as if I was a windmill
and you the only wind.

This towering illusion –
when you fall, my soulmate,
you will find my wreckage
lying in all directions.

Birds eat from me
the parts you also like in me.
I soar, we dig together
to reach the sky.
I race ahead of the sky
in order to find you.

The river's arm is long.
It steals from trains
striving for the station.
I am like an idiot –
each time taking the same train.
This is not a trap.
I simply tripped over myself.
What's wrong with you,
you cursed misery?
Don't leave me
in wretchedness with you.

Two lonely people –
I'm like a starving man
with my last breath
trying to bite myself.
We will not reach each other.
Between us there are seven skies.

I hang my watch upon a wishing time-line,
let water woo your image,
and fold it in quiet turns.
The sun has drunk it up.
Every season, from now on,
will be rainy.

Like fingers flicking
a heart of glass,
your breath is like a child
about to put a flame
into the mouth of the tale
and so discover fire.

Since you are the birds,
they cannot fly outside my lungs.
I hammer coathooks onto light-rays
before our lives eventually become
a soil for wild plants.

I try to free myself
from what enslaves me.
I am a nail that's driven
into the plot of a tale.
Don't set your hopes on me
for I am close to breaking.
I will be abandoned.
May rust protect me from eternity.

I cut the distance short to hug you
even through sea and mountain,
but I am utterly hopeless
unable to sweep yearning
from the streets of my soul,
from my being.
Do not die today.
Die every day.

I will plant a new rose every day
till you've become a garden.

**Exercise**

In your absence
I used to train myself at hefting words
until the muscles of my heart swelled up
becoming harsh.

# Sparrow

Oh, little Sparrow
flapping with your wings,
may my heart fly with you.
Let it beat with you.

Take from me what you need
of grain and grasses.
Hold heaven in your beak
and hang it from branches.

Many green leaves await,
many leaves fly and fly.
Oh, little bird,
teach me to be
as light as leaves.

# Words

Words whose skirts do not fly up
to reveal the meaning at the core of life
and make us cry,
are merely words.

Words that won't undo their tops
to breast-feed passers-by
till they're satisfied,
are merely words.

Words that don't betray their meaning,
but use instead absurdity,
are merely words.

Words that would never cause
a back-street conflagration,
for all their synonyms and antonyms,
are merely words.

## With Me

With me, you'll be alone
like a ring on heaven's finger,
or in the heart of the lake
you will simply be a stone.

With me, you'll lose yourself.
I will sit in between you and me
to watch the Earth
melting without breath.

Don't bring me roses.
Don't say a single word.
You are alone with me.

# BILAL AL MASRI – POET

Bilal Al Masri was born in Tripoli, Lebanon in 1974. He is a self-taught person, active in the Lebanese literary community and known throughout the Arab world. He has published four poetry collections and has selected poetry translated into French in 2023. He has written three novels and two plays as well as children's stories, which were translated into English in Canada.

Selected poems have appeared in six anthologies, including in English and Polish. He has received four different awards including the "Zheng Nian cup" national prize in China in 2023.

His most recent poetry collection is "Crushing His Head with the Stone of Memory," part of Ishraqat – a series on Arab Poetic Voices that is being curated by the iconic Syrian poet, Adonis.

Bilal is married to Sonia Essa (of Palestinian heritage) and they have two children together, Waheeb, aged twelve, and Ghazle, aged ten.

# DR ANBA JAWI, MBE – TRANSLATOR & EDITOR

Born in Baghdad, Dr Anba Jawi studied Geology at the University of Baghdad, one of a generation of pioneering women geologists in Iraq, and gained her PhD from UCL London. She worked in the refugee sector for more than 20 years and was honoured with an MBE on the Queen's birthday list in 2004 for her services. Anba writes and publishes in Arabic and English. A chapter from her novel *The Silver Engraver* was included in the TLC *Free Reads Anthology* (2019) and two chapters were produced in a chapbook published by Exiled Writers Ink (2021). Together with Catherine Temma Davidson, Dr Anba Jawi co-translated and co-edited the anthology *The Utopians of Tahrir Square*, published by Palewell Press in 2022. Together with Catherine Temma Davidson, she co-translated and co-edited the poetry collection *Please Don't Kill All The Poets* by Adnan Mohsen, published by Palewell Press in 2024.

# DR MOHAMAD HAJ MOHAMAD – TRANSLATOR

Dr Mohamad Haj Mohamad is an associate professor and a graduate of Keele University, Staffordshire, England. Born in Syria, Dr Haj Mohamad earned his BA in English literature at the University of Aleppo, Syria, and his PhD at Keele University, UK.

His thesis addressed the works of Ezra Pound, the USA-born poet of early modernism. He taught American and English poetry and other literary subjects at Syrian and Jordanian universities.

In addition to his academic duties, Dr Haj Mohamad supervised many cultural events. He directed plays, organized poetry symposia and other facultative activities. His first poetry collection *Shehrezad and Songs of Existence* speaks about frustration, hope, and beauty. His love of history and art illuminates his poetry and testifies to his continuing search for beauty.

# PALEWELL PRESS

Palewell Press is an independent publisher handling poetry, fiction and non-fiction with a focus on books that foster Justice, Equality and Sustainability. The Editor can be reached on enquiries@palewellpress.co.uk